BOLD LOVE

DR. DAN B. ALLENDER
DR. TREMPER LONGMAN III

A DISCUSSION GUIDE
BASED ON THE BOOK

D1160783

NAVPRESS ◤
A MINISTRY OF THE NAVIGATORS
P.O.BOX 35001, COLORADO SPRINGS, COLORADO 80935

The Navigators is an international Christian organization. Jesus Christ gave His followers the Great Commission to go and make disciples (Matthew 28:19). The aim of The Navigators is to help fulfill that commission by multiplying laborers for Christ in every nation.

NavPress is the publishing ministry of The Navigators. NavPress publications are tools to help Christians grow. Although publications alone cannot make disciples or change lives, they can help believers learn biblical discipleship, and apply what they learn to their lives and ministries.

All Scripture in this publication is from the *Holy Bible: New International Version* (NIV). Copyright © 1973, 1978, 1984, International Bible Society. Used by permission of Zondervan Bible Publishers.

Printed in the United States of America

CONTENTS

INTRODUCTION

What does it mean to love my enemy?—the one who sexually abused me; my spouse who is angry and insensitive; my friend who gossiped behind my back and damaged my reputation; my child who snarls at my offer to go for a walk; the surgeon or service station mechanic who fails to act in my best interest. The list is endless. The book *Bold Love* is about strong and forgiving love—the kind that can deal with tragic and incomprehensible harm like sexual abuse as well as the ordinary and explainable struggles like insensitivity or impatience.

This discussion guide is a companion to that book. It will introduce you to some of the central ideas of the book and give you a chance to discuss and practice them. You don't have to read the book in order to use this guide because each discussion session includes an excerpt from the book. However, this guide only scratches the surface of each concept, so you may find yourself wanting to delve into the book for further explanation and examples. In addition, the book contains many ideas not covered in this guide. At least, the group leader should read the relevant chapters of the book before each session.

Because most of us have busy schedules, this guide

is designed so that as participants you don't have to prepare anything in advance of your discussion sessions. Instead, each session includes some ideas for taking home what you've learned and putting it into practice. During the discussions, you can jot your thoughts and responses in this guide.

Each session contains the following sections:

A warm-up question. You'll be coming to sessions with your mind full of the events of the day. To help you start thinking about the topic at hand, and also to help you get to know the other members of your group, we often begin with a warm-up question. Don't skip it; you'll find that you appreciate what you'll learn about each other and yourself.

Text. This material is adapted from the book *Bold Love.* Someone in the group can read this aloud, or you can take a few minutes to read it silently. Each session tells you where to go in the book to read more about that session's subject.

Discussion questions. These will help you understand what you've read and consider how it relates to your own experience and struggles. Also, the discussion will help establish a bond of trust with others to help you grow with the issues.

During the week. In this section you'll find ideas for trying what you've learned. Feel free to do something different.

HOW DO YOU LOVE AN ENEMY?

LEADER: You may want to begin with some or all of the following approaches:

- ◆ As a group, ask God to use this study to make each of you more like Christ.
- ◆ Read aloud some or all of the introduction on pages 5-6 (you could take turns reading paragraphs).
- ◆ Introduce yourselves.

Next, ask one or more people to read aloud the following excerpt from the book *Bold Love*. Ask group members to think about this question as they read along: What thoughts and feelings in these stories do you identify with?

DILEMMAS

Sherry's father hated women. Every time she was with him, she was subjected to his tirades about her "frigid" mother and his "lesbian" customers. She was his one and only "pretty lady," and she carried the burden of his cruelty upon her weary, guilty shoulders. When she finally suggested to him after twenty years of being his surrogate spouse that his attitudes toward women, including her, might be damaging her soul, his well-chosen words cut like a cold dagger: "I thought you cared about me. I guess you're just a dyke like all the rest."

What would it mean for Sherry to forgive her father for years of abuse? Jesus said to "turn the other cheek." She'd already done that hundreds of times, yet she was getting pummeled beyond recognition by her father's verbal blows. She wanted to forget she even had a father. But the Bible said she was supposed to love him.

Patrick's wife was still the love of his life. After fifteen years of marriage, she could make him laugh like no one else, and as a hostess for his clients, she stole the show. Everyone loved a party when Penny was there. She had that magic touch, and Patrick was so proud of her. But whenever he tried to talk to her about what he really felt, how much he wanted her for more than a laugh, how she hurt him and the kids with the endless public performances that stole her heart from them, she blew up. "Oh, don't be ridiculous! What do you want from me, anyway? You can be such a baby." Sometimes, she'd apologize later, but nothing ever really changed. The cycle of pain kept cutting deeper into Patrick's heart.

Patrick knew all about "forgive and forget." It was the only solution. He loved his wife. But could he really go on like this for the rest of his life? What about the kids? It was becoming harder and harder to overlook Penny's caustic replies and soul-numbing contempt. Forgiving and forgetting wasn't getting their family anywhere. So what did God expect of him? What was love for a wife who just didn't care?

Jane's phone was ringing again. It was probably Carol. It seemed like it was always Carol. She was really having a rough time of it — had been for as long as Jane could remember. She needed someone to talk to, and Jane did love her. Carol could be so sweet, and she always listened to what Jane had to say and tried to follow her advice. But the resentment was building inside Jane. "How can she be so self-centered? All we talk about is her problems. What about me? What about a give-and-take relationship? I'm really getting sick of this."

But "love covers a multitude of sins." Sure, Carol could be selfish, but she was really struggling. Shouldn't

Jane be a little more forbearing? She didn't want to resent Carol, but it was getting harder to forgive the daily ringing of the phone. She wasn't feeling much love anymore. What did God really want from her, anyway? She just wanted out. *(Taken from chapter 1 of* Bold Love, *pages 23-24.)*

1. What thoughts and feelings in these stories struck chords in you?

2. Briefly describe one situation you are facing where you're finding it hard to love someone (unless you did this in response to question 1). Why does it seem so hard?

LEADER: Each person should have a chance to respond to question 2. In order not to run out of time, ask group members to limit their stories to two minutes.
Read the following paragraphs aloud.

IS LOVE IMPOSSIBLE?

Love may be necessary for survival, but daily existence seems to make love impossible. Love is essential, but it seems maddeningly unreasonable. It is both what we desire and despise, wait for and ignore, work toward and sabotage.

Could it really be true that love, without divine intervention, is impossible? *(Taken from chapter 1 of* Bold Love, *page 28.)*

3. Do you agree or disagree with this last sentence? Why?

9

LOVE AND FORGIVENESS

How do we really view the idea of forgiveness? What have we done to derail the kind of forgiving love that enters the fray of betrayal and brokenness with a bold, courageous desire for the kind of reconciliation that redeems all the Evil One's efforts to destroy?

Forgiving love does not merely get one through tough times or give purpose to the daily grind of life. *Forgiving love is the inconceivable, unexplainable pursuit of the offender by the offended for the sake of restored relationship with God, self, and others.* It is the kind of love that has fallen on hard times in our self-oriented, take-care-of-yourself age. Few, if any, question the importance of love, but the idea that we need to love others rather than ourselves is more readily thought to be a symptom of a sickness called codependency.

Women are often told they love too much or love the wrong kind of man. Love is now a diagnostic criteria for measuring mental health. If you love the unlovable, let another person's desires take precedence over your own, or even worse, love someone who has hurt you, then you are likely love addicted, codependent, and emotionally unhealthy.

Without question a common perversion of love is dependent, demanding, and soulless in its giving, so that, in fact, it ceases to be love. What an odd thought—love that is not loving. It is obvious that what we call love might be little more than a slightly veiled, self-interested demand for appreciation and respect. And what we call forgiveness may be a self-aggrandizing—or its tragic opposite, a self-destroying—avoidance of the offense in order to achieve an end other than biblical reconciliation. The difference between love and forgiveness and their counterfeits is obviously complex and bewildering.

The premise of this book is simple: *I will not live with purpose and joy unless I love; I will not be able to love unless I forgive; I will not forgive unless my hatred is continually melted by the searing truth and grace of*

the gospel. True biblical forgiveness is a glorious gift
for both the offender and the offended. Few of us
have ever understood what the Bible really means
when it speaks of forgiveness, and clarity won't come
immediately in the early chapters of this book. But
keep reading. Forgiveness is even harder than we think
it is—but infinitely more life-giving. If love offers life,
forgiveness enables love. *(Taken from chapter 1 of* Bold
Love, *pages 29-30.)*

4. Have you ever given or received "love" that you
   now consider unhealthy? What do you think was
   wrong with it? For instance, was it either of these?

   ◆ "A slightly veiled, self-interested demand for
     appreciation and respect."
   ◆ "A self-destroying avoidance of the offense in
     order to achieve . . ." (security, a feeling of right-
     eousness, safety from conflict).

5. How do you feel when you hear about "the kind
   of forgiving love that enters the fray of betrayal
   and brokenness with a bold, courageous desire for
   the kind of reconciliation that redeems all the Evil
   One's efforts to destroy"? What goes through your
   mind when you hear that?

6. What one or two questions about love or forgiveness
   would you like God to answer during the coming
   weeks of this study?

FINDING STILLNESS

"Could it really be true that love, without divine intervention, is impossible?" Fortunately, divine intervention
is available. Take a few minutes as you close to ask God

for it. If some group members are unaccustomed to praying aloud, start simply. During a minute of silence, participants can think about the hard-to-love people in their lives and about the questions they have about love. Then each person should have a chance to ask God for one thing, such as an answer to a question or a change in some relationship. If the group members are comfortable praying together, you can loosen up this format to allow for spontaneous thanks and requests.

DURING THE WEEK

As you go through your week, watch for times when love seems hard or next to impossible. Ask yourself why it's such a challenge to forgive and open your heart without lashing out, carrying a half-conscious grudge, or sweeping something under the carpet.

The book *Bold Love* includes much more than can possibly be covered in a discussion guide. You don't have to read the book in order to participate in the discussion, but the book will flesh out many ideas. For instance, the introduction and chapter 1 clarify the meaning of love and its connection with forgiveness and also challenge several popular notions of love. Chapter 2 addresses one barrier to love: the anguish of living in a fallen world where choices are hard and abuse is so common. Reading these chapters will give you a better background for this session and the next.

Session 2 deals mainly with chapter 3 of the book, which explains how that barrier to love can be overcome. Reading chapter 3 ahead of time would be an excellent preparation for session 2.

STUNNED BY GRATITUDE

Love is a lot of work. Why bother? This session examines something that has to happen inside us before we'll be willing to bother loving.

1. Briefly describe a time when you felt deeply grateful to someone for something. What were the circumstances? What sparked your gratitude?

LEADER: Read the following paragraphs aloud. Ask participants to follow along and circle statements they identify with.

WHY SHOULD WE LOVE?

Gratitude for forgiveness is the foundation for other-centered love. . . . A stunned and grateful heart is free to love because it has been captured with the hilarious paradox that we are unlovely but loved, and unable to love but free to try without condemnation. . . .

If this is true, then why do so many seem to love so

poorly? Part of the answer is that few are that silent or that grateful to God for the work of the Cross. Instead, most of us are somewhat irritated with God that He has not done more to resolve our struggles with an outstanding mortgage debt—or with the debt that is owed to us by a parent who abused us. To be honest, few Christians are that overwhelmed by the power of the gospel to save our souls from hell, because the unpleasant consequences of living in a fallen world feel too much like a hell in which God refuses to intervene. *(Taken from chapter 1 of Bold Love, page 43.)*

2. a. Which statements did you circle, and why?

   b. Did you have trouble understanding or identifying with anything in this excerpt? Explain.

3. Jesus said, "He who has been forgiven little loves little" (Luke 7:47). So, if we want to become people who love greatly, we must become more aware of how much selfishness and damage God forgives us for every day.
   How does that idea strike you? What do you feel when you hear that?

4. What do you say inside yourself when you are caught doing something wrong? Do any of the following sound like you? *(Some statements were taken from chapter 3 of Bold Love, page 70.)*

   ◆ "If you only understood the unbelievably tough decisions I am called to make every day, you would not hold me accountable to make any more. Indeed, if you truly understood how hard

14

I've labored to make every godly and honoring decision, you would get off my back."

♦ "If you only understood how much I've been hurt, neglected, and abused, you would know that God requires little (or next to nothing) from me."

♦ "When God did not intervene to stop the abuser, He lost any right to require me to do anything. He owes me; I owe Him nothing."

♦ "I'm hopeless; I'll never learn to love. All I do is hurt people. I might as well give up."

♦ "Oh, my! I had no idea how much damage I was doing to this person. I'm shocked – speechless. There's no excuse for this."

♦ "I can't remember the last time I was caught doing something wrong."

If none of these sounds like your internal message, how would you express it?

LEADER: Read the following excerpt aloud. Ask participants to think about whether they have experienced what is described here.

STUNNED INTO SILENCE

How does the gospel alter our hearts, especially for someone who has had orthodox familiarity with the gospel for eons without ever being deeply changed? How do we embrace the truth so that our hateful hearts are overwhelmed by gratitude? The answer, in part, is to be silenced by the gravity of our condition.

Silence is required for deep change to occur. Once we are silent, it is possible for us to look into God's eyes and discover His response. We anticipate fury, yet what we find is fondness; we expect, at least, cool indifference in light of our disregard and anger, yet what we discover is passionate joy at our return to a relationship with Him.

God's disruptive and scandalous response to our hatred transforms fury into gratitude and deadness into life. The silence that deeply changes our heart is the hush that comes when we are caught in our hatred and found to be without excuse. The experience of being captured by eyes that searingly penetrate to the depths of our hurt and fury intensifies our shame and terror at first. Over time, however, the experience of being seized by God's strong and tender sorrow (in the light of what we deserve) stuns us beyond words and opens our heart to freeing gratitude. . . .

What is the kind of silence that brings about a lengthy look into the eyes of God? It is the silence evoked by surprise. . . .

Godly silence always yields stunned joy. It is our raw foolishness in the face of God's unyielding power, His relentless purpose, and His glorious presence that silences us. His unnerving goodness stuns us. He simply does not respond to my hatred as I fear He will, as I have experienced in countless other relationships before, as I know He should! His discipline, though painful, eventually yields a harvest of joy. His exposure of my sin, though penetrating and shame-inducing, leads to an embrace that is sweeter than meringue. *(Taken from chapter 3 of* Bold Love, *pages 65-66, 71, 75.)*

5. Have you ever experienced either of these? Tell something about your experience.

   ◆ Being silenced by the gravity of your condition. (Has this happened within the last year?)
   ◆ God's disruptive and scandalous response to your hatred. (Have you ever even been aware of hating God or someone else?)

16

6. Many people find that what is described in the previous excerpt is largely beyond their experience. Which statements do you have trouble identifying with? What questions does the excerpt raise for you?

LEADER: Read the next section aloud.

THE THRILL OF SALVATION

Even if I have known little or no love in life, as a Christian I am face to face and flesh to flesh intertwined with love incarnate. Love is before me, like a wall, like a deep cut on my hand. It is unforgettable; it is inflamed within me; it is a shrill, silent, noisy, still voice that captures my deepest and most superficial thoughts. . . .

I am constrained by His presence to love, or at least to anguish over my failure to love, and then to humble myself by putting on those fine robes, the gleaming ring, and the well-fitted sandals. [See Luke 15:22.] Why does He not make me pay? It would be so much easier if I could just suffer a few years in penance; but alas, He not only rejoices at my return, but He invites the whole neighborhood to celebrate with us. He charms me and compels me without force or pressure to rejoice, to be grateful for His wild and wonderful imposition. I can no more escape Him or His call than I can refuse, at least for long, to breathe or to stop my heart from beating. . . .

This is the framework for offering forgiveness and reconciliation to others. God in Christ models for us a wild, reckless, passionate pursuit of the offender by the offended for the sake of the most shame-free party known to man. If one has been forgiven much, then one will learn to boldly pursue through every possible means the one who has done him harm. The path will

17

not be like any other journey. It is a path marked by quiet repentance, stunned joy, and passionate celebration. It is a path that leads both forgiver and forgiven into the heart of God. *(Taken from chapter 3 of* Bold Love, *pages 85, 86.)*

7. How does the previous excerpt make you feel?

   ◆ Inspired—I want to experience this passion, but I haven't yet.
   ◆ Frustrated—I don't know what the author is talking about.
   ◆ Joyful—I've tasted a little of this grateful compulsion to love.
   ◆ I don't feel anything.
   ◆ Other (name it):

8. *(Optional)* Luke 7:36-50 and 15:11-32 both depict people stunned into gratitude. Look at one of these stories together. In the former, Jesus points out that a prostitute who knows that God has forgiven her severe sin loves Him more than a Pharisee who feels he's been forgiven for only minor sins. In the latter, Jesus contrasts a younger son who is joyfully amazed by his father's pardon with an older son who is unaware that he even needs his father's pardon.

   Do you find yourself identifying more with the grateful, forgiven woman/son or with the loveless, indignant man/son?

FINDING STILLNESS

Such rare stillness will likely not happen, in most cases, by simply reading words in a book or effortfully trying to become silent by meditative exercise. The silence of being caught is an existential moment that can be prayed for (Psalm 139:23-24) and prepared for (1 Corinthians 11:31, 2 Corinthians 13:5), but it cannot be summoned like a butler called to come to our service. *(Taken from chapter 3 of Bold Love, page 68.)*

Take a few moments of silence to think individually about how deeply aware you are of how much you need God's forgiveness. Tell God your thoughts. You may choose to do the following:

◆ Ask Him to give you that experience of being stunned by who you are and who He is.
◆ Ask Him to show you what keeps you from feeling deeply grateful more often.

DURING THE WEEK

Take time to look at Luke 7:36-50 and 15:11-32. Ask God to show you why you have cause to be joyfully grateful for His forgiveness.

Chapter 3 of *Bold Love* lays out the idea of being stunned by gratitude in much more detail. It would be extremely valuable to read that chapter in its entirety. It's hard to grasp the ideas in this session without reading the examples in the book.

Chapter 4 introduces the concept you'll discuss in session 3: Love is spiritual warfare.

LOVE IS WAR

When we're stunned by gratitude for the way God has loved us, we'll begin longing be like Him. We'll also want to join His side in the war against evil. We were created to be spiritual warriors. But what's the battle?

1. In a couple of sentences, briefly describe a recent time when you were aware that you were engaged in a spiritual war. (It's okay to say you've never been aware of that.)

LEADER: When the next excerpt is read aloud, ask participants to assess the view of spiritual warfare presented here.

FACING THE WAR

One reason we are so easily blinded to the vital importance of forgiveness is our penchant to deny that we are in a war. The Evil One wants us to question God. He desires, even more, for us to ignore the need to grapple with God or the world in which we live. *We will see the importance of forgiveness as a central category in relating to others to the extent that we see every relationship enmeshed in a war that leads to a taste of heaven or hell.* If we understand the battle we are engaged in and the nature of the wounds we experience, forgiveness is seen as the foundation for comprehending the goodness of God and the only hope for restored relationships with others. The premise of this chapter is that forgiveness becomes more necessary to the degree the damage of living in a fallen world is faced.

What is the nature of the war that pervades every relationship? In simple terms, the war is a battle with sin. Every relationship is strained by the burden of sin. If carefully examined, every relationship has ample reason to fold under the constant weight of harm. . . .

The sounds of war are never far. The low rumble of artillery and the ear-shattering wail of jet fighters overhead are a common, daily intrusion for those with ears to hear. The blood of soldiers is flowing daily in what is truly the mother of all wars — the fight between good and evil, the war between God and the prince of darkness. . . .

Unfortunately, the metaphor of war seems like a television cliché that has lost its punch because most lives are utterly disconnected from the carnage of a true war. Christians seem to see the war of God against evil in terms that are limited to moral issues — pre- or extramarital sex, pornography, abortion, and secular humanism. Other Christians who see the war in terms of social injustice view the battle in light of poverty, class struggles, racial prejudice, and sexism.

I utterly agree with both perspectives, although few who battle one war seem to accord the other much validity. But notice that in both perspectives, the fight is not perceived as an issue of the heart or in context of relationships. Both externalize the war in terms of an "ism" (capitalism, secular humanism), which is a philosophical system of living, or a group of faceless, nameless enemies who oppose life (abortionists, freedom of choice activists, or bigots). Again, I should not be read as minimizing the war against philosophical tenets or social, political, economic, or religious groups that deny the gospel. But if this is the only real battle, then the war is not only extremely far from where many live, it is largely irrelevant to the lives of Christians who are called to arm themselves with the armor of God.

There is a war and it seems that many Christians are not only on the back lines, but also uninformed as to the nature of the battle. The war is against the powers of the prince of darkness. There are many who may read the last sentence and, in a knowing and perhaps condescending manner, agree the real war is against the forces of evil. Paul says, "For our struggle is not against flesh and blood, but against the rulers, against the authorities, against the powers of this dark world and against the spiritual forces of evil in the heavenly realms" (Ephesians 6:12).

There are many who believe the real war is exclusively supernatural; therefore, when a person struggles from depression, disease, or destructive social ills, the only legitimate focus is to do battle with demons through the work of deliverance. Deliverance ministries abound and offer Christians the opportunity to be freed from almost any manifestation of sin, struggle, or spiritual battle through binding the effects of the demonic and removing their presence and their deleterious effects. The consequence of this is to remove the battle to a sphere of existence that is alien to the daily, ordinary, normal struggles of most people.

If the war is seen as an "ism" or a faceless group, then the average person is disconnected from the fight. If the battle is doing or receiving "deliverance," then most people do not need to be rescued from the immediate attack of Satanic forces or are not "gifted" to fight directly with the powers of evil. Again, I would be misread if I were seen as categorically castigating all deliverance approaches to life's problems. My concern is that few seem to know the battle that rages around them even in enjoyable moments and pleasant interactions, and few seem to be aware of the wounds that result from their daily engagements.

The real war is supernatural and is against the forces of evil arrayed against God and His people. The commander-in-chief of the evil forces is the prince of darkness, and his cohorts include legions of rebellious angels who hate God. But the war doesn't rage "out there" in heavenly realms far removed from the daily grind of life. The powers of darkness work for the destruction of good through all ideologies, social structures, institutions, and events. To put it simply, the Evil One works through the basic building block of all ideologies, social structures, institutions, and events—namely, people. In other words, he works through the dynamics of one person relating to another, attempting to accomplish his destructive goals.

Through one human being relating to another philosophical and societal structures take their shape. The terrain of the eternal war is the battleground of relationships. The battles may be of immediate and enormous consequence, like the choice to have an abortion rather than face the shame of an angry father's stare, or more long-term and seemingly insignificant, like the choice to chew on a spicy piece of gossip about a coworker. In either case, no one makes a moral, ethical, or social decision without engaging in a contest of supernatural proportions. *(Taken from chapter 4 of* Bold Love, *pages 88, 89-92.)*

Do not be overcome by evil, but overcome evil with good. (Romans 12:21)

2. What do you think of the way spiritual warfare is defined in the excerpt from the book?

3. In session 1, you described a relationship in which you are finding it hard to love. Where do you see spiritual warfare going on in that situation?

4. How do you suppose prayer fits into one's love-war strategy?

5. Does seeing love as spiritual warfare affect the way you'd like to approach any of your relationships? How?

FINDING STILLNESS

Since God is in charge of strategy, tactics, equipment, training, and morale in your war of love, it's worthwhile to check in with Him regularly. What would you like to tell your Commanding Officer right now? Do you need guidance? Guts? A change of heart? Take a few minutes to tell God how you're feeling about the battle you're engaged in and to ask for His help.

DURING THE WEEK

Try to be aware this week of the spiritual battle you face as you deal with the people in your life. You might take some time to write down your thoughts about the battle as you see it. Or go for a walk and talk with God about it. If your relationships are a battleground, it might be worth half an hour consulting with God about them.

Chapter 4 of *Bold Love* sketches the war of love in more detail, particularly the war against hatred and lust. Chapter 5 surveys the biblical background of warfare and God as a Warrior. Chapter 6 discusses four qualifications of a warrior; in session 4 you'll examine two of those qualifications.

QUALITIES OF A WARRIOR

Love is spiritual warfare, and chapter 6 of *Bold Love* describes four qualities crucial to a spiritual warrior. You'll examine two of them in this session.

1. What people, things, or ideas are important enough to you that you are willing to live, suffer, or die for them?

LEADER: While this excerpt is read, participants should think about this question: Do I live for heaven, or do I live demanding that life be like heaven?

COURAGE

We will not be free to love until the cliché "this is not our home" becomes real. It is sewn into the fabric of our being that we will courageously defend whatever is most dear to our hearts — a woman will, at all costs, protect her young; a man will defend against intruders who attempt to harm his family or home. In a similar way, we will take heroic risks to protect whatever is the treasure of our heart, be it a child, a home, a country, a philosophy, God. . . .

How would you answer the questions, "Do I live for heaven?" or "Do I live demanding that life be like heaven?" Your answers will determine what you will spend your life fighting for.

What most of us spend the energy of our lives warring against is reality—the fact that life is awful and the truth that this world is not our home. I am surprised when the effects of a fallen world impinge on my life. I know people die. I know tragedies occur. I am aware that people have affairs and marriages end. But for some reason, I am stunned when a good friend dies or a child of parents I know is diagnosed with a fatal disease. I am shocked when someone I've worked with in a ministry context has an affair and leaves his wife. Though I face sin and its debris every day, I somehow assume that when I leave my office, I can drive away from sin's sorrow.

When I see the debris of the storm in my friends, family, and my mirror, I am forced to see that the ravages of sin are inescapable. If I am surprised by sin in my life or in others, I am operating according to a tragic assumption about life. *If I do not anticipate the regularity and tragedy of sin, I unavoidably come to believe this world is my home.* It may be near impossible to release the lie, "This is my home; I deserve life, love, and liberty," but no one will choose a path of sacrificial, courageous love if this life is either all there is or is nearly as good as the next. One will choose the better only if the present is faced as it is—not worth living for, but worth dying to change. *(Taken from chapter 6 of* Bold Love, *pages 139-140.)*

2. In what ways do you live demanding that life be like heaven?

3. When you think about all the tragedies, betrayal, and suffering around you, how do you tend to feel? (Numb? Outraged? Despairing? Bewildered?)

4. What do you think of the idea that life is awful and this world is not your home?

5. What might you do differently if you just accepted the fact that this life is awful?

> LEADER: As the following excerpt is read, have participants evaluate the view of God presented here.

CONVICTION

Cancer, like sin, feeds on the healthy cells of the body. It sucks the life-giving nutrients away and destroys the body from the inside out. It is silent, malignant, and subtle. It may not even be diagnosed until the body is almost destroyed. In time, it ravages beauty and saps hope and joy. It brings death and sorrow. . . .

How do I feel about my father's enemy, cancer? If I were a warrior and my father's enemy were to come into my presence, I would kill it. I long to wrap my hands around its neck and squeeze the life out of that which has sucked the life out of so many.

Is that God's attitude toward His enemy? We often hear the biblical-sounding phrase, "God hates the sin, but loves the sinner." The dilemma is that sin cannot be abstracted from the sinner. Without the blood of Christ, what is sent to hell—the sin or the sinner? Hell is not a housing project for abstractions, but a place where

29

sinners are left to live out the consequences of their unpardoned sin.

For example, how is it possible to hate adultery without hating the adulterer? What is adultery? Is it merely sexual infidelity—sexual relations with the wrong person? Or is it a profound breaking of a covenant of trust, which cancerously devours the soul and relationships? If it is the latter, then adultery is a big deal. Sin is cancer personified; sin involves rebellious behavior, but it is more than a measurable, objective violation of the standards of God.

Many will agree sin is more than an abstraction or a mere behavior to be condemned; it is a force, a malevolent energy in the soul that blights and destroys. So what of the question, "Doesn't God love the adulterer, the gossip, the denier, the enabler, and so forth?" Doesn't He hate the sin, but love the sinner?

The answer is both yes and no. Indeed God loves the sinner, but He also hates the sinner. In Proverbs 3:32, we read, "The LORD detests a perverse man." The passage does not divide the man from his actions. . . .

We are to join God in His hatred of both the sinner and the sin, beginning with the sinner with whom we are best acquainted—ourself. The marvel of grace is that we are all inflicted with the same cancer as those we are called to love. We are called to be opthomologists—eye doctors who see a disease in the eye of another and are so committed to removing that speck of cancer that we knowingly undergo the same surgery to remove the mass in our eye in order to remove the disease in the other. The covering of grace enables us to know our disease is still rampant, but we will never die. Therefore, with a piercing hatred of our sin, we are called to announce tenderly and strongly the prospect of a cure to others. This kind of engagement with other sinners involves a hatred of whatever will destroy life and beauty.

Proverbs further says, "To fear the LORD is to hate evil; I hate pride and arrogance, evil behavior and perverse speech" (8:13). Most Christians I speak to find it inconceivable that they are required to hate. Normally we are encouraged not to think of God as a stern, angry father who beats us when we are bad, but as a warm, caring grandfather who does not want us to sin because He knows it will hurt us, but when we violate His will, He loves us anyway. God is love and wants us to love just as He loves.

Yet ask most Christians, "Does God hate cancer?" The answer is usually yes. Ask, "Does God hate arrogance and pride?" The answer is often a blank stare. If He hates the internal working of sin, not just the external manifestation of sin, then in a sense, He hates me because I am, at times, haughty and arrogant.

Is God stern and angry, or warm and kind? In a sense, He is both. He is a father who delights in His child, so He therefore disciplines His child with a rebuke (Proverbs 3:11-12). Another contemporary image is the oncologist. He is a cancer specialist who will do anything to destroy that which destroys. He will surgically cut away flesh; He will burn out cells through radiation; and He will poison them with chemotherapy. The treatment is, at times, brutal and appears cruel, but the result is profoundly life-enhancing and lovely. Discipline, though it often feels like a judgment that exiles and abandons us, is a labor of love that beautifies the heart through the disruptive touch of a severe mercy. *(Taken from chapter 6 of* Bold Love, *pages 148-150.)*

6. What do you think of the view of God presented here?

7. How do you respond to the idea that you need to hate the evil in yourself and others enough to take drastic measures against it?

8. How might taking this stance affect some of your current relationships?

FINDING STILLNESS

By now you may be getting used to praying together. Your leader may want to choose a specific topic for group prayer or open up the time for you to tell God what's on your minds. Talk with God about any difficulties you feel in seeing this world as temporary or in hating sin in yourself and others. Can you thank Him for hating the evil in you and the world? Ask Him to do whatever it takes to cultivate courage and conviction in each of you.

DURING THE WEEK

Frequently this week, ask yourself the question, "Am I living for heaven?" What do your actions show?

Chapter 6 of *Bold Love* clarifies the ideas of courage and conviction; it also explains two other qualities of a warrior: *calling* and *cunning*. In session 5 you'll discuss material on cunning from chapters 6 and 8. (Most of chapter 8 addresses revenge, which you'll talk about in session 7.)

SHREWD AS SNAKES, INNOCENT AS DOVES

A love warrior must be stunned by God's mercy, committed to a Kingdom beyond this world, and gripped by a loathing for evil. This session explores another surprising quality of an effective warrior.

1. Would someone who knows you describe you as cunning? Why do you say that?

LEADER: Ask participants to consider, as they listen to the next excerpt, whether or not they find its argument convincing.

CUNNING

When our Lord sent His disciples out for their inaugural evangelism campaign, He told them to "be as shrewd as snakes and as innocent as doves" (Matthew 10:16). . . .

An excellent example of this passage is the prophet Nathan. God told him to rebuke King David for the sins of murder and adultery. It was well understood during that day that no one should make a king unhappy. . . .

33

The consequence for disturbing a king was death. Imagine, then, how Nathan felt about not only bringing a few sad feelings David's way, but in fact, being the agent to expose his shame of murder and adultery.

Nathan told David a story. He told about the evil deeds of a cruel and enormously rich land owner who stole another farmer's only lamb. The story moved David, and he called for judgment on the man. Nathan, at that point, said, "You are the man!" (2 Samuel 12:7). Nathan tricked David into pointing the finger at himself. Nathan, through cunning and wisdom, gave David enough rope to hang himself and also escaped a dangerous mission with his own neck.

The methodology will likely be different in every situation, but the principle is the same: Be wise and use the situation to the best advantage in order to achieve God's larger purpose. Jesus commends this type of manipulative shrewdness. The dishonest servant is honored because he cuts a deal with those who owe money to the master. He knows he will gain favor in the eyes of his peers and be granted honor after the master fires him. The Lord recognizes this when He tells the disciples that "the people of this world are more shrewd in dealing with their own kind than are the people of the light. I tell you, use worldly wealth to gain friends for yourselves, so that when it is gone, you will be welcomed into eternal dwellings" (Luke 16:1-16). . . .

[A] crafty Christian exposed her husband's outrageous attacks by giggling. For years, she bore his contemptuous barbs by withdrawing into a sullen funk. Occasionally, she would lash out, rant and rave, then descend into a deeper depression, but the effect merely added fodder to his smoldering rage. The battle lines were drawn, and it was trench warfare. The wicked equilibrium was shattered when she began to see the sinfulness of her sullen funk. The process was far messier and more deeply personal than I can imply by words, but her good, redeemed heart was eventually pierced by the reality that seemingly reasonable behaviors, given her verbally abusive husband, were actually fueled by her own rage.

Over time, she began to experience deep sadness over her sin and the sin of her husband. Redemptive sorrow eventually increased restorative passion, and she began to deal with his accusations without contempt for herself or for him. At times, she wept, but the tears were not coated with an angry heaviness that required a response from her husband. They were tears of pain that were gentle and open. At other times, his puffed-up cheeks and reddened face reminded her of a blowfish, and she could not help but giggle. In both cases, her tender, non-punitive passion infuriated him worlds more than her depressive funk. At least her funks could be patronized and blamed on a deficiency in her. Her passion, on the other hand, invited him to deal with his sin, and for that, he hated her with a new passion that dwarfed his past dislike of her. His hardness and cruelty became clearer to his friends and church, and eventually he was compelled to look at his life.

The reason for craftiness and surprise is simple: The fallen human heart is continually attempting to predict and control. As long as a person can be categorized and explained, he can be anticipated and dismissed. "You know ol' Frank. He's a religious fanatic. Did you really expect him to go to the office party?" It is a sad thing that Christians are often so highly predictable.

. . . Craftiness, which is innocent with the pure desire of seeing God's glory reign supreme, is required to cut through defenses and open the enemy's fortress door. Frontal attacks are obvious and may be easily deflected; surprise attacks may open the door to the heart by breaking down the expected categories of response. Dressing the troops in red coats and sending them out to battle in regimented lines is not only arrogant, but foolish.

Our craftiness shows itself, fundamentally, in *choosing to do good to those who have done us harm*. It is alerting the enemy to our capacity, willingness, and resolve to use power and then offering peace—certainly, not offering peace at any cost nor conditions of peace that lead to the potential of damaging others. Rather, cunning is *an outmaneuvering of the enemy for the purpose of rendering him powerless, in order to offer him the opportunity for restoration.* *(Taken from chapter 6 of* Bold Love, *pages 152-154.)*

2. Do you find the argument in favor of godly cunning convincing? Why, or why not?

3. a. What seems hard about becoming innocently crafty?

   b. What solutions can you suggest for those obstacles?

LEADER: Read the following excerpt aloud.

Do not be overcome by evil, but overcome evil with good. (Romans 12:21)

THE POWER OF GOOD

Only redemptive goodness has the ability to destroy evil and express the wonder of the work God has done in our life. This is indeed an odd thought. We experience the opposite from the playground to the board room. A heart of mercy seems to invite abuse; intimidation invites (cold) respect. The offering of goodness to those who have done us harm seems absurd. Indeed, it is utterly out of kilter with what makes sense.

It would be logical to avoid someone who has harmed you, or at least, to do all that is necessary to limit his ability to do harm again. It would make even more sense, if it were safe, to destroy someone who did you harm, so that harm could not be perpetrated again. Instead, the Bible tells us to love our enemies, turn the other cheek, and do them good. Why? What is the point behind such odd commands?

Evil knows the ways of evil. Evil has its own perverse logic and rationale, even if it appears to be illogical and unreasonable. What evil cannot comprehend is goodness. Goodness offers life; evil seeks death. Goodness walks in light; evil slinks in darkness. Evil may be contemptuous of the good, but it is equally baffled by its power and beauty.

Good draws forth rage from evil because evil desires to get the good to operate from the same principles of warfare. Good does not (ultimately) succumb to the principles of evil. Instead, it conquers by the force of redemptive beauty. Goodness is not weak or sentimental. It is a force of power that is designed to surprise, supplant, and shame evil. *(Taken from chapter 8 of* Bold Love, *page 204.)*

4. What struck you as significant in this view of good and evil?

5. Did you find the argument convincing? Explain.

6. What might it look like for you to do good to those who are doing evil to you these days? Try to brainstorm some creative, cunning ideas for each other.

FINDING STILLNESS

Openhearted cunning may seem a million miles away from where you are now. You may want to start your prayer time by asking God to give you wisdom and innocence. Also, lay out your situations before Him and ask for cunning strategies for handling each one. You could pair off with one other participant to do some concentrated praying about just your personal situations.

DURING THE WEEK

Look for opportunities to be cunning in love. Sometimes emotions cloud our thinking during a situation, and we think of what we should have done only when it's too late. If this happens to you or if you just find yourself going blank when you think about a strategy of love, talk with God about the problem. Is fear of the other person's response or fear of embarrassing yourself hindering your clear thinking?

Chapter 6 of *Bold Love* clarifies how to acquire cunning. Chapter 8 adds more thoughts on cunning and also addresses the issue of session 7: revenge.

But first, session 6 returns to the idea of forgiveness. What is it, and what isn't it? You'll look at two questions about forgiveness: Does it mean peace at all costs? And, do I have to enjoy being around this person? You'll get a much wider perspective on these and other questions by reading chapter 7 of the book.

FORGIVENESS

We raised the subject of forgiveness in session 1, then we seemed to drop it with all the talk of hoping for heaven, hating evil, and acquiring cunning. Now we can think about forgiveness in the context of a war fought by soldiers gripped with gratitude.

1. Think of someone who has hurt you badly. What has been (or is) the hardest part for you of forgiving that person?

LEADER: Chapter 7 of *Bold Love* examines in greater detail what biblical forgiveness does and doesn't mean. (Is forgiveness a one-time event? Does it mean not feeling hurt anymore? Does it mean forgetting the incident? Does it mean becoming close friends with the one forgiven?)

CANCELING THE DEBT

The Scriptures use many metaphors and stories to illustrate the meaning of forgiveness. A central theme is that an incomprehensible debt owed to the Master has been mercifully canceled. The canceled debt frees the debtor from eternal imprisonment, shame, and destitution. The only debt that remains is to offer others a taste of redemptive love (Matthew 6:9-15, 18:21-35). *To forgive another means to cancel the debt of what is owed in order to provide a door of opportunity for repentance and restoration of the broken relationship. (Taken from chapter 7 of* Bold Love, *pages 159-160.)*

2. Consider again the person who has hurt you. What debt does he or she owe you (for instance, what has that person stolen from you)?

3. According to God's law, a thief must either pay back the debt or be sold as a slave to pay the debt (Exodus 22:3). When you cancel the debt, you agree not to demand immediate payment or punishment. What does it cost you not to demand immediate payment or punishment for the debt you just named?

LEADER: Notice that we speak of not demanding *immediate* payment. The rest of this session and session 7 will explore why. As you read the next excerpt, ask participants to consider what they think of conditional forgiveness.

DOES RECONCILIATION MEAN PEACE AT ANY COST?

The driving motive behind forgiveness is the hope of reconciliation. . . .

Reconciliation is costly for both the offended and

the offender. The offended forgives (cancels) the debt by not bringing immediate judgment and termination of the relationship, as might be reasonable and expected, given the offense. Instead, mercy is offered in order to invite the offender back into the relationship. The cost for the offended is in withholding judgment and instead offering the possibility of a restored relationship. The cost for the offender is repentance. *Biblical forgiveness is never unconditional and one-sided.* It is not letting others go off scot-free, "forgiven," and enabled to do harm again without any consequence. Instead, forgiveness is an *invitation* to reconciliation, not the blind, cheap granting of it.

Jesus says, "So watch yourselves. If your brother sins, rebuke him, and if he repents, forgive him. If he sins against you seven times in a day, and seven times comes back to you and says, 'I repent,' forgive him" (Luke 17:3-4). Jesus makes it clear that forgiveness is conditional. We are not to rebuke unless a sin has been committed, nor are we to forgive unless true repentance has occurred. This strikes many Christians as wrong. Are we not to forgive, irrespective of the other person's response? Didn't the Lord forgive those who crucified Him when He said, "Father, forgive them"?

An important question must be asked: When the Lord forgave those who crucified Him, did He grant to each of them, at that moment, a place of eternal intimacy with His Father? I don't think so. I believe He was freeing them from the immediate consequences of touching God for the purpose of destroying Him. They deserved the kind of immediate judgment that occurred when the Ark of the Covenant was touched in the Old Testament. Jesus was only forestalling their judgment in asking for them to be forgiven. The only redemptive forgiveness offered in that scene was to the thief who was crucified beside Jesus. The thief's response of repentance and faith granted him reconciliation and intimacy with the Father.

The point for us is crucial. Reconciliation is not

to be withheld when repentance—that is, deep, heart-changing acknowledgment of sin and a radical redirection of life—takes place in the one being rebuked. Nor is reconciliation (the offer of restoration and peace) to be extended to someone who has not repented. *Forgiveness involves a heart that cancels the debt but does not lend new money until repentance occurs.* A forgiving heart opens the door to any who knock. But entry into the home (that is, the heart) does not occur until the muddy shoes and dirty coat have been taken off. The offender must repent if true intimacy and reconciliation are ever to take place. That means that cheap forgiveness—peace at any cost that sacrifices honesty, integrity, and passion—is not true forgiveness. *(Taken from chapter 7 of* Bold Love, *pages 161-163.)*

4. So what do you think about this idea of forgiving someone only as an invitation until he repents?

5. What would this conditional forgiveness look like in one of your relationships?

LEADER: Two stories dominate this next excerpt. The first illustrates the point that real forgiveness involves passion. The second depicts the pain of daring to long for change. Ask participants to underline anything they identify with.

HOW CAN I WANT A RELATIONSHIP WITH SOMEONE WHO IS SO HARMFUL?

A woman asked me in a wide-eyed state of disbelief, "Are you saying I should want a relationship with a father who continues to leer at my breasts and make lewd comments?" My answer was yes and no. Is she to want a relationship with him as he is? Of course not. Is she to hunger for a relationship with him, deeply desiring him to become the man that God intended for him to be if he repented? The answer is yes. We are to hunger for what redemption and the work of repentance might do in our life and in the lives of those we love and those we hate.

A passionate desire for reconciliation with one transformed by God's grace will enable us to offer true forgiveness. Forgiveness that is offered without the deep desire for the offender to be restored to God and to the one who was harmed is, at best, antiseptic and mechanical and, at worst, hypocritical and self-righteous. *Forgiveness is far more than a business transaction; it is the sacrifice of a heartbroken Father who weeps over the loss of His child and longs to see the child restored to life and love and goodness.* Forgiveness always involves the strongest emotions of the soul. It is always beats with a fervor for the offender and the relationship to be restored to beauty.

One man told me of the battle to restore a marriage he had broken through an extramarital affair. He said the hardest part of restoring the relationship was his wife's absence of hurt and anger. She was kind and condescending, pleasant and vacuous, forgiving and self-righteous. It appeared that her forgiveness had no purpose beyond "doing what's right," fulfilling an obligation rather than canceling a debt for the hope of heart-thrilling restoration. Though her forgiveness was robotic and passionless, all their friends marveled over her strong faith and balanced emotions. He longed for the passion of a soul that wrestled with the wrong done and then offered the same passionate embrace of forgiving love. . . .

I counseled a woman who had been barbarously and ritualistically abused by her father and mother. After many months of work, she began to explore her feelings toward her father. At one point, she asserted that she would, and could, never forgive her father for his evil cruelty. I asked her this question: "What would you do if God gave you the choice between pushing a button on your left, which when touched would utterly destroy your father at this minute, or a button on your right, which would lead to radical, deep repentance and the kind of change that would make him the father God intended him to be?" She sat stunned for a long time. Her shock turned to silent, teary rage. She glared at me for almost twenty minutes. After what felt like an eternity, she said, "You have put me in a terrible bind." I agreed.

Her next words were startling. She said, "If I push the button on the left, then I am saying I am as evil as he is. But if I push the button on the right, then I am admitting I really want him to be my father. And I am far more afraid of allowing my heart to feel desire and longing than I am of being evil." She had spent most of her life killing the desire for her dad to be a true father. The idea of pushing the button on the right, with its implications, was far more terrifying than pushing the button on the left. (*Taken from chapter 7 of* Bold Love, *pages 163-165.*)

6. What did you underline, and why?

7. Do you resemble any of the following examples?

  ◆ The wife who deadened her hurt and anger so that "she was kind and condescending, pleasant and vacuous, forgiving and self-righteous."
  ◆ A person who chooses to press the left button, instantly frying the enemy.
  ◆ Someone who is willing to endure the pain of hurt and longing for closeness with a changed person.

8. Why is it hard for you, in one of your current relationships, to choose to long for repentance and restored intimacy? What does that longing cost you?

FINDING STILLNESS

During a minute of silence, each of you can think about people with whom you are unreconciled. To whom would you like to be restored? What obstacles do you see? Then talk with God about those situations. One simple approach would be for everyone to make one request for God to do something in a situation.

DURING THE WEEK

Set aside some time to consider one of your relationships in the light of what you've been discussing. (It would be enormously helpful to read chapter 7 of *Bold Love* in its entirety.) What will it cost you to offer forgiveness and long passionately for change?

Talk with God about that cost. You might look at Matthew 18:21-35 or Luke 7:36-50. Don't try to pummel yourself into obedience (it's hard to make yourself long for something passionately). Instead, tell God about your hurt, your anger, your frustration—whatever thoughts and feelings surface as you think about canceling the debt.

Many of us presume that revenge has no place in the war of love. Session 7 will examine that presumption. Chapter 8 of the book treats the subject much more fully.

REVENGE

❖

Canceling someone's debt means withholding restitution and punishment, but it also means waging a
cunning war against evil. This sounds like withholding
revenge and then taking revenge. Is that correct?

1. How do you feel when you think of desiring revenge
   against someone who has wronged you? (Gleeful?
   Horrified? Torn between the two?)

LEADER: As the next excerpt is read, ask participants to think about the connection between love
and revenge.

IS REVENGE EVER RIGHT?

*Bold love is the tenacious, irrepressible energy to do good in
order to surprise and conquer evil. . . .*

Love now sounds a lot like revenge. Love may
demand change; love may bring consequences for a
failure to change; love may withhold involvement until
beauty is pursued; love may hurt the other for the sake

of a greater good. But many may say this sounds very similar to hatred and vengeance! . . .

I am amazed how many Christians view revenge as intrinsically evil. I asked one man if vengeance was ever good. He answered, "It is the most vile of human desires. It goes back to the tribal demand of an eye for an eye. As Christians, we've gone beyond tribal vengeance to an ethic of love that offers the cheek, rather than requiring the repayment of an eye." Again, there is a measure (small as it may be) of truth in his words. We do operate on an ethic of love, but his assumption is that love and vengeance are in opposition.

The same disturbing assumption sees an inherent contradiction between mercy and justice. I asked the same man why he believed he was more righteous and pure than God. He was stunned. He argued vociferously that he loved God and did not presume he was better than God. At one point during his protestations, I quietly said, "Vengeance is mine, says the Lord." His expression softened, and he remarked, "I see your point." If vengeance is inherently perverse, then God is wrong for claiming it as His domain. . . .

The key to illicit revenge is making someone pay — now! — for a real or perceived crime without any desire for reconciliation. Illegitimate revenge is assessing and executing final judgment today without working to see beauty restored in the one who perpetrated the harm.

Vengeance, at times, can be illegitimate, but it is not inherently wrong. Vengeance is part of the character of God and is not in contradiction with His love and mercy. Revenge involves a desire for justice. It is the intense wish to see ugliness destroyed, wrongs righted, and beauty restored. It is as inherent to the human soul as a desire for loveliness.

. . . Revenge is, in part, a desire to see someone pay for the wrongs that have been done to us. The desire for restitution is the basis of our justice system. If I take something from you, I should not only give it back, but repay you for your loss. Revenge invites restitution. Repayment of the harm done is always a symbol of what is ultimately required of us all—our life as payment for sin. . . .

A commitment to beauty—that is, to doing everything we can to birth good and destroy evil—is the heartbeat of biblical revenge. The person who does harm must pay for his sin, now and perhaps later. Without payment, arrogance—like a weed—will grow, and a disregard of God—like a thicket—will become thicker and more impenetrable. Punishment, in the form of legal consequences, church discipline, biblical rebuke, or supernatural discipline, is both a warning and an opportunity for repentance, as much for the believer as for the unbeliever. . . .

Paul says without equivocation, "Do not take revenge, my friends, but leave room for God's wrath, for it is written: 'It is mine to avenge: I will repay,' says the Lord" (Romans 12:19). In a final sense, revenge of judgment pronounced and executed is beyond us. Why? Paul uses a fascinating phrase to explain why we are not to seek it today. He tells us to "leave room for God's wrath." . . .

It is my opinion that our final vengeance, no matter how well it has been thought through or planned, would never be enough to cover every offense. I asked one enraged victim of a spousal affair what she would do to her husband if she could make him pay. She said, "I would scream at him for hours, then I would shoot him." I told her that she was far more lenient and generous than God would be. She had never read Isaiah 25:4-12, so I asked her if she would be willing to let him lie face down in his dung, slowly drown, and be trampled underfoot by teams of horses. She was disgusted with my suggestion and said outright that I was a strange and violent man. When I argued that I was merely reflecting the essence of what God would eventually do to all those whose citizenship is with Moab, she was startled and miffed.

She wanted her husband to pay, but she really did not want him to pay too severely. Her "mercy," though, was less merciful than it was squeamish. If God hates sin so deeply that He is willing to severely punish it, then perhaps He does not take too kindly her own manifestations of arrogance. We naturally tend to limit the extent of our desire for vengeance on the basis of an innate knowledge that we deserve the same. Consequently, final vengeance taken today is anemic and puny. It tries to squeeze God into a form of punishment that is substantially less than what is deserved.

Paul is encouraging Christians to wait because the fireworks will be far more spectacular when they all go off at one time. Lighting one cherry bomb today and then a Roman candle next week tends to water down the boom. Do we really want to be part of a spectacular show? If we do, then we are to wait until the Lord arrives before we take our best shot at revenge. He does promise that we will have our opportunity to participate. *(Taken from chapter 8 of* Bold Love, *pages 185, 186, 187, 189, 192, 193.)*

2. a. According to this argument, what revenge should we pursue in this life, and why?

    b. What revenge should we not pursue in this life, and why?

    c. What do you think of this argument? Are you convinced that there is legitimate revenge we should hope for and even pursue? Explain.

3. What are some situations in which you are longing for justice?

The hand of the LORD will rest on this mountain;
　　but Moab will be trampled under him
　　as straw is trampled down in the manure.
They will spread out their hands in it,
　　as a swimmer spreads out his hands to swim.
God will bring down their pride
　　despite the cleverness of their hands.
He will bring down your high fortified walls
　　and lay them low;
he will bring them down to the ground,
　　to the very dust. (Isaiah 25:10-12)

4. How does it affect you to know that evildoers have the fate described in Isaiah 25:10-12 awaiting them? How might it affect the way you deal with evildoers in your life?

5. What might it look like for you to pursue the destruction of evil and the flowering of beauty in someone you are finding hard to love?

FINDING STILLNESS

Pair off with a partner. This time, pray for justice in your partner's life. Can you pray with the passion God has for the destruction of evil?

DURING THE WEEK

Take some time to talk with God about the justice you long for in some relationship. What would you like God to do? What should you do in the meantime?

　　The concept of revenge is fleshed out much more thoroughly in chapter 8 of *Bold Love*.

　　Session 8 looks at some practical counsel for loving

boldly from chapter 12 of the book. You may want to read all of chapters 9–12, which give a great deal more practical information, especially about different ways of loving different kinds of people.

COVERING OVER SIN

By now we may be picturing ourselves armored and riding off to slash cunningly at the cancer in our friends and relatives. This final session should provide a balanced perspective.

1. Think of a time when someone confronted you for doing something wrong. Recall how that person handled the confrontation and how you felt in response. Now, tell the group one thing that was good about the way the person confronted you *or* one thing you think was unwise, unhelpful, or unloving.

LEADER: Chapters 9–12 of *Bold Love* offer a lot of practical advice for loving different kinds of people: the mocker (evil person), the fool, and the simpleton (normal sinner), as Proverbs describes them. The following is a sample about when and how to confront.

Tell participants to underline statements in this excerpt, as they listen, that seem to be key features of covering over sin.

COVERING OVER, COVERING UP

Our basic stance toward sin should be an utter clarity and honesty about the offense, without any mood of a cover-up. . . . While we are observing data and forming and testing deductions, our mood must be to cover over sin.

Covering over sin involves the choice consciously and purposely to turn our eyes away from the transgression, without ignoring or denying the damage. Peter tells us, "Above all, love each other deeply, because love covers over a multitude of sins" (1 Peter 4:8). . . . Love does not attempt to stir up trouble, nor does it hatefully attack in order to demand change. Proverbs states, "Hatred stirs up dissension, but love covers over all wrongs" (10:12); and "He who covers over an offense promotes love, but whoever repeats the matter separates close friends" (17:9).

Covering over sin involves the choice to believe the best in the other. It acknowledges the failure, but focuses on the other aspects of goodness that can legitimately be enjoyed. . . . Our critical generation seems to know little about affirmation's power to call forth a nobility in the heart. Covering over sin enables all that can be admired in another to surface and flourish.

Covering over is never based on denial or fear. Whenever either factor is involved, the cover over has turned to a cover-up. Covering over never involves pretense. The leaders of God's people were condemned for making sin look less sinful than it is (Jeremiah 6:14, Ezekiel 13:10-11). Pretense, in this case, is excusing sin ("He didn't mean to do it. Given his background, he really couldn't help it") or pretending the wound did not hurt ("If I got upset every time someone attacked me, I wouldn't get anything done at all"). Neither attitude reflects true forgiveness or love.

The process of covering over without covering up sin involves the choice to limit our response based on *data, opportunity,* and *calling.*

Data. When we cover over sin, we make a con-

54

scious choice to wait, prayerfully and patiently, for the right moment to deal with an observable pattern of sin. . . . The simple person might easily write off an individual failure as an anomaly, but a full-fledged, well-developed pattern is more difficult to deny. A wise person resists the temptation to pluck young fruit and, instead, waits for sin to ripen on the vine. He covers over sin until the data of a significant pattern of failure is ripe and irrefutable.

Once we've been in a relationship long enough to recognize a specific action as part of a destructive pattern, it is imperative to expose our heart to God as an offering for His service. Part of one's conversation with God ought to involve questions of *character* ("What about my life might call into question my sincerity, integrity, or commitment? Does my friend know I struggle for him?"), *content* ("What do I need to say, and what is best to leave for another time?"), *methodology* ("What approach will best gain a hearing? How will I invite the person to interact about the data?"), *follow-up* ("Once I've spoken, am I willing to pray, talk, or deal with the struggles that come up? If I am poorly received, am I committed to a friendship, irrespective of what is said or done?"). . .

Timing. Covering over sin involves waiting for the right opportunity for interaction about a pattern of sin. There are few times when the sin is so clear and so important that it bears public exposure (Galatians 2:11-21). Wisdom waits for the pregnant moment when words can penetrate and expose with tender grace and lithe strength. Generally, the opportune moment is in private and also soon after the offense. The offense should be recent enough that its glow is still silhouetting the mountain and can't be easily ignored. I am not implying other data that confirms a pattern is wrong to bring up, but in most cases, the immediate example ought to take the bulk of conversation.

Calling. Finally, we should cover over sin unless we are called by God to deal with it directly. The calling to confront will likely be laced with confusion.

There are many levels of friendship, intimacy, and commitment. You may ask, "At what point am I called to risk a relationship by opening the door to a difficult conversation?" . . .

Don't confront if you love to confront. I think God prefers reluctant draftees to overeager zealots in the area of confrontation.

A person who stirs up strife is a fool. The calling to confront should be resisted and ignored until the burden is unbearable and God's voice is clear. I truly believe calling is a supernatural set-up where God draws the line in the sand, clasps His hands around your neck, and pulls you into the ring.

Let me illustrate the relationship between data, opportunity, and calling. . . . I was telling a story at a gathering of friends and said that I had been involved in some enterprise for about three years. My wife quickly said that it was only two years. I felt hot with shame and anger. I remember thinking, *Why must she correct the story so that it is precisely accurate?* I wanted to say something about "my wife, the calendar," but I held my tongue, felt my hurt, and chose to go on with the story without a jab at her. After our friends departed, I desperately wanted to let her know that I felt hurt and angry, but she had enjoyed the evening. I did not want to detract from her enjoyment, and I believe in my wife; she is not a mean-spirited woman who normally takes her anger out on me in a subtle, public fashion.

A few days later, the same thing occurred again. I let it pass. The next day in a normal conversation, with no one else around, she corrected several details as we made plans for the evening. I finally asked her if she was aware of how often she was editing my stories. She was stunned. We pursued the data, and eventually acknowledged significant patterns of harm in our relationship. She felt like I dominated conversations and, at times, was thoroughly bored with my rambling. It was a painful, but highly significant, conversation. She apologized for the hidden anger, but stood her ground regarding my demeanor in certain gatherings. I, in turn, did not back away from the hurt, but I took responsibility for my insensitive domination. As so often occurs in any confrontation, there are issues for both parties to face. In this case, we were both at fault and profited from seeing our failure of each other in a context of love. Covering over sin buries the sin in grace and waits to see if and when it should ever be discussed. *(Taken from chapter 12 of* Bold Love, *pages 299-301, 302, 304-305.)*

2. What did you think of this husband-wife confrontation? (What seemed wise to you? What would you have done differently? Why do you think this would or wouldn't work in your relationships?)

3. How would the difference between covering over and covering up sin apply to a situation you are facing? (What would covering over look like? What would covering up look like?)

> LEADER: If you have time, wrap up your discussion with a look at this excerpt from the epilogue in *Bold Love*. Ask group members to underline statements they want to remember as they leave the group.

BOLD LOVE

I am most concerned about our potential to disguise meanness and revenge deceitfully under the cloak of bold love. I was recently told about an acquaintance, Jan, who was "boldly loving" her mother. When Jan began to face the harm she had suffered in relationship with her family, she cut off contact with her mother, claiming her mother was too damaging to relate to on any basis. A friend questioned the wisdom of her extreme response, and Jan refused to talk with her, claiming her friend was in denial. She became a one-woman SWAT team against anyone who challenged her definition of love.

The dispute with her mother was over the issue of past abuse: Did Jan's deceased father abuse her or was Jan lying? Her mother refused to believe her, so Jan cut off all communication. Jan's mother is a weak, indulgent woman who refuses to deal with any ugly, messy problems. Her refusal to address life as it is, is wrong. But there are strands of data that indicate her mother has a real concern for Jan and a willingness to creep slowly toward facing truth. Should Jan refuse to talk with her mother until she acknowledges the past abuse? I cannot answer definitively, but I suspect bold love is being used (or misused) in this situation as a bludgeon to make her mother pay for the years of uninvolved, nonprotective mothering.

The person who chooses to love boldly must remain open to more data and feedback in order to know how to deal wisely with the offender. The cost will be an enormous struggle with doubt and confusion that results from refusing to come to premature certainty through arrogant self-assertion. The person who boldly loves will remain tentative in his or her direction without losing the courage to move forward. In the use of extreme measures, there will be even greater thoughtfulness, time, and interaction with others before one moves. A defensive, closed, angry retort—"You just don't understand. This is repentance for me to cut off ties with my mother"—likely indicates a heart motivated by revenge rather than by mercy and grace.

I wish the process of loving were clearer and more simple. In many cases, it is. It is merely offering someone a cup of cold water in the name of Christ. Other times, love involves all the sophisticated planning and technology of a war. One central point must be underscored: *Unless we have made it a lifestyle to offer cups of cold water, we will not be able to engage properly in the warfare that bold love requires. (Taken from the epilogue to* Bold Love, *pages 311-312.)*

4. What statements in this final passage seem especially worth remembering?

5. For you, what would be involved in pursuing a lifestyle of offering cups of cold water? (To whom might you offer "water," and what might that "water" be?)

6. How has your view of love changed as you've been using this guide? How have your dealings with others been affected?

FINDING STILLNESS

How have you changed as a result of this study? Tell God what you're grateful for. Also, ask Him to clarify for you what the next steps will be in your various situations.

DURING THE WEEK

You probably still have many questions about love. If you haven't already obtained a copy of *Bold Love* to read in its entirety, consider doing so.

Many answers will come only as you experience more and more of that surprised silence before God, the gratitude for His forgiveness, the hatred of evil, and the hope for heaven.

Who are the people (even one or two) with whom you can slog through the mud side by side? Make it a priority to find a few people willing to share support and feedback in your joint pursuit of bold love.

HELP FOR LEADERS

This guide is designed to be used in a group of from four to twelve people. Because God has designed Christians to function as a body, we learn and grow more when we interact with others than we would on our own. If you are on your own, see if you can recruit a few other people to join you in working through this guide. You can use the guide on your own, but you'll probably long for someone to talk with about it. On the other hand, if you have a group larger than twelve we suggest that you divide into smaller groups of six or so for discussion. With more than twelve people, you begin to move into a large group dynamic, and not everyone has the opportunity to participate.

The following pages are designed to help a discussion leader guide the group in an edifying time centered on God's truth and grace. You may want to have one appointed person lead all the sessions, or you may want to rotate leadership.

PREPARATION

Your aim as a leader is to create an environment that encourages people to feel safe enough to be honest with themselves, the group, and God. Group members should sense that no question is too dumb to ask, that the group will care about them no matter what they reveal about themselves, and that everyone's opinion is as valid as everyone else's. At the same time, they should know that the Bible is your final authority for what is true.

As the group leader, your most important preparation for each session is prayer. You will want to make your prayers personal, of course, but here are some suggestions:

- ◆ Pray that group members will be able to attend the discussion consistently. Ask God to enable them to feel safe enough to share vulnerable thoughts and feelings honestly, and to contribute their unique gifts and insights.
- ◆ Pray for group members' private times with God. Ask God to be active in nurturing each person.
- ◆ Ask the Holy Spirit for guidance in exercising patience, acceptance, sensitivity, and wisdom. Pray for an atmosphere of genuine love in the group, with each member being honestly open to learning and change.
- ◆ Pray that your discussion will lead each of you to obey the Lord more closely and demonstrate His presence to others.
- ◆ Pray for insight and wisdom as you lead the group.

After prayer, your most important preparation is to be thoroughly familiar with the material you will discuss. Before each meeting, be sure to read the text and answer all of the questions for yourself. You will find it enormously helpful to read the corresponding chapters in the book *Bold Love* ahead of time. Each session tells which chapters to read. This will enable you to answer questions group members might raise.

Choose a time and place to meet that is consistent, comfortable, and relatively free from distractions.

Refreshments can help people mingle, but don't let this consume your study and discussion time.

LEADING THE GROUP

It should be possible to cover each session in fifty minutes, but you will probably find yourself wishing you had two hours to talk about each group member's situations. As you conduct each session keep the following in mind.

Work toward a safe, relaxed, and open atmosphere. This may not come quickly, so as the leader you must model acceptance, humility, openness to truth and change, and love. Develop a genuine interest in each person's remarks, and expect to learn from them. Show that you care by listening carefully. Be affirming and sincere. Sometimes a hug is the best response—sometimes a warm silence is. You can start putting bold love into practice in the ways you deal with participants.

Pay attention to how you ask questions. By your tone of voice, convey your interest and enthusiasm for the question and your warmth toward the group. The group members will adopt your attitude. Read the questions as though you were asking them of good friends.

If the discussion falters, keep these suggestions in mind:

- ◆ Be comfortable with silence. Let the group wrestle to think of answers. Some of the questions require thought or reflection on one's life. Don't be quick to jump in and rescue the group with your answers.
- ◆ On the other hand, you should answer questions yourself occasionally. In particular, you should be the first to answer questions about personal experiences. In this way you will model the depth of vulnerability you hope others will show. Count on this: If you are open, others will be too, and vice

versa. Don't answer every question, but don't be a silent observer.

◆ Reword a question if you perceive that the group has trouble understanding it as written.

◆ If a question evokes little response, feel free to leave it and move on.

◆ If discussion is winding down on a question, go on to the next one. It's not necessary to push people to see every angle.

Ask only one question at a time. Often, participants' responses will suggest a follow-up question to you. Be discerning as to when you are following a fruitful train of thought and when you are going on a tangent.

Be aware of time. It's important to honor the commitment to end at a set time.

Encourage constructive controversy. The group members can learn a great deal from struggling with the many sides of an issue. If you aren't threatened when someone disagrees, the whole group will be more open and vulnerable. Intervene when necessary, making sure that people debate ideas and interpretations, not attack each other's feelings or character. If the group gets stuck in an irreconcilable argument, say something like, "We can agree to disagree here," and move on.

Be someone who facilitates, rather than an expert. People feel more prone to contributing with a peer leader than with a "parent" leader. Allow the group members to express their feelings and experiences candidly.

Encourage autonomy with the group members. With a beginning group, you may have to ask all of the questions and do all of the planning. But within a few meetings you should start delegating various leadership tasks. Help members learn to exercise their gifts. Let them start making decisions and solving problems together. Encourage them to maturity and unity in Christ.

Validate both feelings and objective facts. Underneath

the umbrella of Scripture, there is room for both. Often, people's feelings are a road map to a biblical truth. Give them permission for feelings and facts.

Summarize the discussion frequently. Summarizing what has been said will help the group members see where the discussion is going and keep them more focused.

Don't feel compelled to "finish." It would be easy to spend an entire session on one or two questions. As leader, you will be responsible to decide when to cut off one discussion and move to another question, and when to let a discussion go on even though you won't have time for some questions. If there are more questions than you need, you can select those that seem most helpful.

Let the group members plan applications. The "During the Week" sections are suggestions. Your group should adapt them to be relevant and life-changing for the members. If people see a genuine need that an application addresses, they are more likely to follow up. Help them see the connection between need and application.

End with refreshments. This gives people an excuse to stay for a few extra minutes and discuss the subject informally. Often the most important conversations occur after the formal session.

THE FIRST SESSION

You or someone else in the group can open the session with a short prayer dedicating your time to God.

It is significant how much more productive and honest a discussion is if the participants know each other. Therefore, you might want to allow some extra time in this session for people to elaborate on their answers to question 2. But be considerate of other participants by asking a talkative member to bring his or her story to a close.

At some point during the session, go over the following guidelines. They will help make your discussion more fruitful, especially when you're dealing with issues that truly matter to people.

Confidentiality. No one should repeat what someone shares in the group unless that person gives permission. Even then, discretion is imperative. Be trustworthy. Participants should talk about their own feelings and experiences, not those of others.

Attendance. Each session builds on previous ones, and you need continuity with each other. Ask group members to commit to attending all eight sessions unless an emergency arises.

Participation. This is a *group* discussion, not a lecture. It is important that each person participate in the group.

Honesty. Appropriate openness is a key to a good group. Be who you really are, not who you think you should be. On the other hand, don't reveal inappropriate details of your life simply for the shock value. The goal is relationship.

Question 4. Many people have been hurt by unloving "love," or by "loving" someone in ways that damaged themselves and others. When we've been victims of what appeared to be forgiveness and sacrificial love, we may be skeptical of those. It's helpful to voice that pain and skepticism so it doesn't subtly confuse the discussion week after week. Chapters 1, 7, 8, and 9 of *Bold Love* address distorted understandings of forgiveness, as well as ways of "loving" that harm others. Sessions 5 through 8 of this guide should be helpful for the wounded, but they may want to read chapters 7 through 9 sooner.

This session raises more questions than it answers because it chiefly gives participants a chance to voice their own questions and past experiences about love. Take those questions seriously by writing them down. You may want to refer to them as you move through the sessions.

Encourage group members who are feeling that love is beyond them. There will be many reasons for hope in later sessions.

SESSION TWO

This may be the most difficult session. It's nearly impossible to understand the idea of being stunned by gratitude until it has happened to us, and we can't make it happen. Chapter 3 of *Bold Love* paints pictures of the shock of conviction and gratitude, but these are too extensive to be reproduced in a study guide. You may want to read the chapter yourself and share with the group what you personally learned from it.

Question 1. This question is intended to help people get acquainted and to establish a warm and open atmosphere. You should answer first, modeling the length and tone of the desired response. Aim for a somewhat light tone this early in the group, but also model honesty. Model brevity. If ten people each take a minute to answer a question, that's ten minutes. If each takes two minutes . . . you see the implications.

Question 3. You may want to answer this one first also. Think about your answer ahead of time. Do you tend to make excuses rather than owning up to being selfish? Do you give up? Do you beat yourself up, hoping that God won't have the heart to hold you accountable? Are you utterly unaware of doing anything wrong? Your honesty will set the standard for your group.

Question 4. If you've read chapter 3 of the book, you'll recognize the fifth response as expressing something of the shock of conviction, of facing the harm we've done without excuse.

Question 5. Many of us haven't been silenced by the gravity of our condition for a long time, if ever. Are you more aware of hatred in your life after reading chapters 2 and 3? Tell the group what you've discovered.

Question 8. You probably won't have time to examine the passages in Luke unless you plan a second meeting. Encourage participants to look at them on their own.

Finding Stillness. You may have to skip a few questions in order to save time for a few minutes of silence.

Because this idea of being stunned may be unfamiliar, time for reflection will be worthwhile.

SESSION THREE

Some of your group members probably come to this discussion with an idea of what spiritual warfare is. Others may have no idea. If the notion of warfare is new to some participants, you might want to present a brief background, such as Ephesians 6:10-20 and 2 Corinthians 10:3-6. Warfare is a consistent theme in Revelation (chapter 12, for instance) — but that is a study in itself. Group members won't need a detailed study of spiritual warfare, but they should know a little of the biblical background.

Once you've read the excerpt, help the group relate love as war to their previous ideas of spiritual warfare. Does it contradict or complement?

Question 4. Both Ephesians and 2 Corinthians reflect the place of prayer in warfare. Praying for the presence of God and against the presence of evil in someone's life is surely an act of love. Praying for wisdom as to how to love someone is also crucial; you'll encounter more on that subject in session 8.

SESSION FOUR

Some in your group may find it hard to accept the assertion that this life is awful. Certainly there is joy to be had, and God showers us with many blessings. But the biblical writers viewed the world with stark realism: "Dear friends, do not be surprised at the painful trial you are suffering, as though something strange were happening to you" (1 Peter 4:12). Many other passages address the idea that we shouldn't depend on this world for satisfaction because we are meant for another. See Romans 8:18-25; Philippians 3:20-21; Hebrews 11:1-40; and 1 Peter 1:1, 2:11-12. That hope for another world is essential; otherwise, facing life's awfulness must lead to despair.

SESSION FIVE

Innocent cunning is not easy to acquire. In the book *Bold Love* we explain the process of growth as a warrior; the necessary qualities aren't developed overnight. In the story of the woman who learned to giggle, you'll notice that she had to examine her own heart and deal with it over a period of time before the wise tactic began to occur to her. Giggling wouldn't have been even possible before her heart was free enough to see the humor and the sadness in her husband's actions.

If group members are frustrated because they can't think of clever ways to overcome evil with good, perhaps you can channel that frustration into a motive to examine their own lives more deeply. We tend to want six easy steps for handling anything, but unfortunately, there are no easy steps to bold love. Together, you may be able to work out responses to each other's situations, because your hearts will be much freer about others' relationships than your own.

SESSION SIX

It may seem strange to think of people who hurt us emotionally as stealing from us. But people steal our time, our self-respect, our enjoyment of self and others, and the blessings and pleasures of life. When people use us, they steal the energy that might have gone into something of value. Other kinds of hurt may reflect more obvious theft: a job promotion, good relations with another person, a reputation (stolen by gossip).

Familiarizing yourself with all of chapter 7 of *Bold Love* will help you field questions about conditional forgiveness. If the group wants to pursue it, you can look at Luke 23:32-43 to discuss the forgiveness Jesus offered to the crucifiers and the thief.

It's not easy to see what withholding reconciliation might look like with someone we live with. It might mean no more than refusal to discuss a subject until the other person ceases to be verbally abusive or owns up to his or her part in a problem. Like all of the principles of bold love, withholding reconciliation can be misused to manipulate and control. If we refuse to become harmless as doves, our serpentine shrewdness is devilish. We'll need to examine our motives continually: Am I really trying to bring out good in the other, or am I merely making him or her pay?

SESSION SEVEN

You should certainly read all that is said about revenge in chapter 8 of *Bold Love*. The concepts in that chapter seem to turn much traditional teaching on its head. Group members may have questions you'll want to handle.

You may find it hard to get to question 5 because the group isn't ready to do more than grapple with the idea of desiring but not seeking revenge. You may want to spend your time identifying relationships in which each of you longs for justice. Many of us learned at an early age not to long for justice because the longing would always be disappointed. We need to allow ourselves to feel that longing in order to revoke revenge from a stance, not of resignation ("I guess I'll have to endure this"), but of confident hope ("I will lay aside my revenge now because I know God will give me justice in the end").

SESSION EIGHT

Some participants may feel frustrated that they're ending this series with more questions than they had in the beginning. Because growing able to love boldly is a process, much of the practical advice about cunning and timing may seem impossible to follow.

Help each participant to identify one positive thing he or she has gained from this series. End on this note of grace and hope: God is delighted when one of His children learns to love a little bit more, even in small things like offering cups of water.

AUTHORS

Dr. Dan B. Allender received his M.Div. from Westminster Theological Seminary and his Ph.D. in Counseling Psychology from Michigan State University. Dr. Allender has been an associate of Dr. Larry Crabb for almost fifteen years and taught with him in the Biblical Counseling Department of Grace Theological Seminary for seven years. He currently teaches and counsels with Dr. Crabb at Colorado Christian University near Denver and travels extensively to present his unique perspective on sexual abuse recovery, counselor training, and Bold Love workshops. He is the author of *The Wounded Heart* and co-authored *Encouragement: Key to Caring.* Dr. Allender and his wife, Rebecca, live in Littleton, Colorado, with their three children, Anna, Amanda and Andrew.

Dr. Tremper Longman III received his M.Div. from Westminster Theological Seminary and his Ph.D. in Ancient Near Eastern studies from Yale University. Dr. Longman is Professor of Old Testament at Westminster Theological Seminary. Dr. Longman has written many professional and pastoral articles and is the author of *How to Read the Psalms* and *Literary Approaches to Biblical Interpretation.* Dr. Longman and his wife, Alice, live near Philadelphia, Pennsylvania, with their three sons, Tremper IV, Timothy and Andrew.